The Wonderful World of

IN
EXAMS

THE WONDERFUL WORLD OF F IN EXAMS

This edition published 2013

First published as F IN EXAMS, BLACKBOARD BLUNDERS and KIDS' KLANGERS

This edition copyright © Summersdale Publishers Ltd 2013

Illustrations by Rob Melhuish and Milla Roelofse

Summersdale Publishers Ltd
46 West Street
Chichester
West Sussex
PO19 1RP
UK

www.summersdale.com

Printed and bound in India by Nutech Print Services

ISBN: 978-1-84953-446-8

Substantial discounts on bulk quantities of Summersdale books are available to corporations, professional associations and other organisations. For details contact Nicky Douglas by telephone: +44 (0) 1243 756902, fax: +44 (0) 1243 786300 or email: nicky@summersdale.com.

The Wonderful World of

IN

EXAMS

Richard Benson

summersdale

Contents

Introduction

Welcome to *The Wonderful World of F in Exams*, a hilarious compendium of our three best-selling collections of schooldays humour.

So, have you got your pencils sharpened, your crib notes written neatly all the way up your arm and your brain in gear? We've all been there, staring at a blank sheet of paper in the eerie silence of the school hall, but not to worry – *F in Exams* brings together a panoply of creative answers from clueless but canny students, and you'll soon be chortling through Chemistry, giggling at Geography and ha-ha-ing at History.

Still traumatised by the ticking clock and 'Put your pens down, please'? Then join us for a voyage back to more innocent times, as *Blackboard Blunders* invites us into the world of childhood -- a world where the spoken and written word come together in new and wholly unexpected ways. Sometimes the mistakes that children make can be not only funny but also truly profound. Take, for example, the earnest and oddly accurate assertion that, 'We have to look after the sky. Polution can spoil it and so can spraying too many arsols.' Others, however, are just plain silly. It is difficult to imagine how the following situation would come about: 'I dident get to sleep mutch because next doors dog was baking all night.' You have been warmed!

Finally, we delve even further into the bizarre and surreal annals of the things children say, with *Kids' Klangers*. Sometimes it's a case of misquoting something they've heard at school, like 'I've been told I can take violence lessons in my music class', and other times it's a brilliant demonstration of innocent but completely accurate logic: 'Have you seen my favourite gloves? They are stripy, and they are shaped like my hand.' This collection of charming and hilarious observations will make you remember just how much fun you had when you were still in short trousers.

What are you waiting for? It's time to throw off your grown-up worries and dive headfirst into *The Wonderful World of F in Exams*!

F IN EXAMS

THE BEST TEST PAPER BLUNDERS

Subject: **Chemistry**

What is a nitrate?

It is much cheaper than a day rate.

Give a brief explanation of the meaning of the term 'hard water'.

Ice

What is a vacuum?

Something my Mum says I should use more often.

What is the process for separating a mixture of chalk and sand?

It is a process called flirtation

What is the process where steam turns into water?

Conversation

What is methane?

Methane is a smelly greenhouse gas which is produced when trees and/or cows are burned.

What is the meaning of the term 'activation energy'?

It's what is needed to get up in the morning.

In a blast furnace it is impossible for aluminium to be extracted from its ores. Why?

Because it is bloomin' hot!

It was predicted in 1988 that tin reserves would only last until the year 2006. However, 18 years later, there are still enough reserves to meet industry demand. Why is this?

Because people are not buying so many tins of baked beans.

Over the last 50 years there has been a significant change in the concentration of carbon dioxide. Give a reason for this.

It's easily distracted.

What are the characteristics of crude oil?

Coarse and rude

Describe the chemical differences between H_2O and CO_2.

H_2O is hot water,
CO_2 is cold water

What is a vibration?

There are good vibrations and bad vibrations. Good vibrations were discovered in the 1960s

The burning of fossil fuels which contain carbon produces a gas called carbon dioxide. Draw a 'dot-and-cross' diagram to represent carbon dioxide.

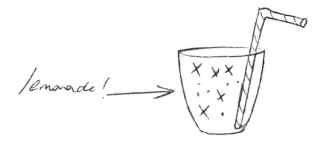

lemonade!

Subject: Biology ....

What is the lowest frequency noise that a human can register?

A mouse

What is the highest frequency noise that a human can register?

Mariah Carey.

Adam cuts his arm. Blood gushes out and is red in colour.
What does this show?

He is not a robot, he's a real boy!

What is a fibula?

A little lie

What is the meaning of the word 'varicose'?

Close by

What does 'terminal illness' mean?

when you become ill at the airport.

State a type of fungus and explain one of its characteristic features.

The Bogey Man. He is green.

What happens when your body starts to age?

When you get old your organs work less effectively

you can go intercontine and

What happens during puberty to a boy?

He says goodbye to his childhood and enters adultery.

Give an example of a smoking-related disease.

Early death

What are the three different types of blood vessels?

Vanes, anchovies and caterpillars.

Karen goes into her garden one morning and finds the leaves covered in a sticky substance. What is this substance?

When the leaves sit in the sunshine they get hot and it makes them sweat.

What is a plasmid?

A high definition television

How is oxygen loaded, transported and unloaded in the bloodstream?

By forklift truck

Explain the concept of homeostasis.

It is when you stay at home
all day and don't go out.

In the Hawaiian Islands there are around 500 different
species of fruit fly. Give a reason for this.

There are approximately
500 varieties of fruit

Explain the word 'Genome'.

It is an abbreviation of the two words:

Gender and Gnome.

Draw a diagram to represent the human body and label the positions of all the major organs including: brain, heart, lungs and kidneys.

Draw a diagram indicating the location of the appendix.

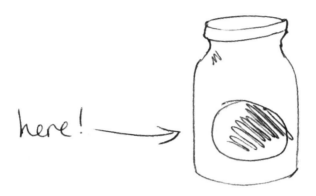

here! ⟶

Below is a diagram of the heart. Please label the relevant sections.

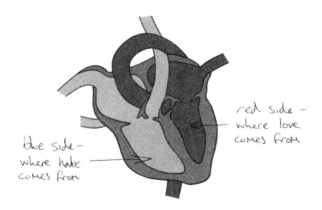

red side —
where love
comes from

blue side —
where hate
comes from

What is a cadaver?

It is a make of a car

What is a fossil?

A fossil is the remains of an extinct animal. The older the fossil, the more extinct the animal is.

What happens to your body when taking a breath?

Your chest gets bigger.

What is the world's largest living mammal?

The woolly mammoth

Subject: **Physics**

Steve is driving his car. He is travelling at 60 feet/second and the speed limit is 40 mph. Is Steve speeding?

He could find out by checking his speedometer.

Explain the word 'momentum'.

A brief moment

What was Sir Isaac Newton famous for?

He invented gravity.

Is the moon or the sun more important?

The Moon gives us light at night
when we need it. The sun only provides
light in the day when we don't.
Therefore the Moon is more important.

Currently, the Sun is in a stable period.
State two balanced forces in the Sun

Page 3 and the footie pages

When a star's life cycle is over there is a possibility it
will become a black hole. Describe a 'black hole'.

Something very dark in the ground and
it looks like this

Many people don't like eating radiation treated food. How could a food scientist prove that radiation treated food is safe?

By eating some!

Name an environmental side effect of burning fossil fuels.

Fire

Describe what happened during the 'big bang'.

A lot of noise.

Why would living close to a mobile phone mast cause ill health?

You might walk into it.

Give the names of two gases that might contribute to global warming.

1. Bottom gas
2. Cow burps

Hannah sprays her new bike purple. The spraying of the bike gives it a negative charge and the paint a positive one. Why is this?

Positive – spraying is easier than using a Paintbrush.

Negative – purple isn't a good colour for a bike.

What is the National Grid?

It is a very large free barbecue in public parks.

What does the National Grid do?

Cooks Sausages to perfection.

What does a transformer do?

It can go from being a robot to a dragster in three seconds.

Give an example of a step-up transformer.

An exercise machine

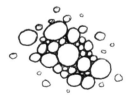

Give a reason why people would want to live near power lines.

You get your electricity faster.

Give three ways to reduce heat loss in your home.

1. Thermal underwear

2. Move to Hawaii

3. Close the door

Mobile phones are very popular. Give one advantage and one disadvantage of owning a mobile phone.

Advantage You can order a takeaway for your school lunch.

Disadvantage Your parents can get hold of you at any time.

What instrument do you use to measure temperature?

A trombone.

Subject: **Geography**

RM
4
TS

Explain the dispersal of various farming types in Britain.

The cows + pigs are distributed in different fields so they don't eat each other

Explain what is meant by the term 'pastoral farming'.

It's a farm run by vicars.

Define the phrase 'commercial farming'.

It is when a farmer advertises his farm on T.V to get more customers.

Define the phrase 'subsistence farming'.

It's when a farmer doesn't get any assistance

Define the term 'intensive farming'.

It is when a farmer never has a day off.

State three drawbacks of hedgerow removal.

1. All the cows will escape.

2. The cows drive into the fields.

3. There is nowhere to hide.

What scale do seismologists use to measure the force of earthquakes?

A very strong one (not glass).

Volcanoes occur on what kind of plate margins?

Hot plates.

What happens at the edge of a destructive plate margin?

It breaks!

'Powerful aftershocks rocked the city, fires burned out of control, streets were full of debris and ruined buildings. At least 30 people were injured.'
Which type of natural disaster is being described in the report?

The end of Big Brother

Name the area of calm at the centre of a storm?

The pie in the sky.

What does the word 'lava' mean?

A pre-pubescent caterpillar

THIS WAY

Explain the meaning of the word 'magma'.

Japanese cartoons.

What is lahar?

A city in Pakistan

Explain the word 'migration'.

Migration is a bad headache.

What is meant by 'a pull factor'?

A big red sports car.

What do we call a person forced to leave their home, perhaps by a natural disaster or war, without having another home to go to?

Homeless :^(

Define the term 'shanty town'.

It is a place where people like beer with lemonade in it.

Define the phrase 'heavy industry'.

An industry that sells tons.

There are many footloose enterprises on an industrial estate.

Define the term 'footloose'.

It means stockings that don't have any feet at the end of them

What was the main industry in Persia?

Cats

The race of people known as Malays come from which country?

Malaria

Name the smaller rivers which run into the Nile.

The Juveniles.

Name six animals which live specifically in the Arctic.

Two polar bears
~~Three~~ Four Seals

Inhabitants of Moscow are called ...

Mosquitoes

Name one of the primary products of the Hawaiian Islands.

Grass skirts and flower necklaces

What is the collective name given to the inhabitants of the Philippine islands?

The Philistines

Name one famous Greek landmark.

The most famous Greek landmark is the Apocalypse

What is the name of the highest peak of the Alps?

The highest mountain is Blanc Munge.

Which artificial waterway runs between the Mediterranean and Red seas?

The Savage Canal.

Name one measure which can be put into place to avoid river flooding in times of extensive rainfall (e.g. in Mississippi).

Flooding in areas such as the mississippi may be avoided by placing a number of big dames into the river

Name one technique used by farmers to improve crop yield.

Farmers mostly increase Crops by irritating the land.

Name two animals native to Siberia.

The lynx and the larynx

What are the Pyramids?

The Pyramids are a large
mountain range which splits
France and Spain

How high is Mount Everest?

Depends how much snowfall it has had since it was last measured.

The Narmada and the Tapi river valleys are said to be old rift valleys. What is a rift valley?

Valleys that have fallen out after an argument.

$2 + 2 = 5$

Subject: **Maths**

Change 7/8 to a decimal.

7.8

Name a regular triangle.

a three - sided triangle.

The Wonderful World of (F) IN EXAMS

Find the angles marked with letters.

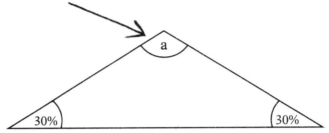

THIS IS THE ANGLE MARKED WITH A LETTER

a

30%   30%

Write two hundred thousand in figures.

two hundred thousand in figures.

What is a six-sided polygon known as?

an empty cage

There are 300 students in Year 10. Mary and Mark want to find out Year 10's favourite colour.
Mary asks 30 people.
Mark asks 150 people.
Mark says 'My conclusions are more likely to be reliable than Mary's'.
Why does Mark think he is right?

Because Mark is a man

A car company is having a sale. A car that was £25,000 before the sale now has 50 per cent off. What is the new price?

Still too expensive.

Expand 2(x + y)

$$2(x+y)$$
$$2(x+y)$$
$$2(x+y)$$
$$2(x+y)$$

Simplify the following equation.

$$\sqrt{\dfrac{5}{5}}$$

$$\dfrac{\sqrt{\cancel{5}}}{\cancel{5}} = \sqrt{}$$

x is inversely proportional to the square of y.

x=3 and y=4

Express x in terms of y.

$$:-x + :-y = :-)$$

What is conditional probability?

Maybe, maybe not

What is the splitting formula?

boy meets girl → boy meets another girl
→ girl finds out about other girl
= the splitting formula.
This is not to be confused with the spitting
formula, that's just antisocial.

What is a random variable?

Someone with multiple personalities

What is a discrete random variable?
Give an example with your answer.

It is a person that hides in the corner at parties. similar to the wall flower but a bit more unpredictable after after a few drinks.

You are at a friend's party. Six cupcakes are distributed among nine plates, and there is no more than one cake per plate. What is the probability of receiving a plate with a cake on it?

Nil, if my sister is invited too.

What is the symbol for Pi?

← Pi!

John and Julie are both strong badminton players. Is it more probable that Julie will beat John in four games out of seven or five games out of nine?

She will win every game.
She is a girl - girls are
better at these things.

How should Julie play to minimise any loss?

Dirty!

Calculate a formula for winning the lottery.

buy a ticket → watch the lottery programme → turn over to Ant and Dec while the boring bit is on → turn back to find out that you have missed the important bit → get cross → ask your parents what the numbers were → they are mysteriously absent from the house and return three weeks later after jetting off round the world after cashing in your winnings

Subject: Business Studies

How do the following companies fund themselves?

a) BBC   phone-in competitions

b) ITV   Same as the above

Explain the phrase 'free press'.

When your mum irons trousers for you.

Explain the word 'wholesaler'.

Someone who sells you whole items, e.g. a whole cake.

Assess Fashion House plc's choice to locate its factory near Birmingham. Is Birmingham the right location for this type of business?

No. People from Birmingham aren't very fashionable.

Paul frequently uses the Internet to research information. Suggest two items of information Paul could locate on the Internet which might help him in running his business.

Item 1: www. how-to-run-a-business. com

Item 2: www. how-not-to-run-a-business. com

Suggest three steps Paul is likely to take when selecting the best candidate for a job.

Step one: **You're hired**

Step two: **You're fired**

Step three: **You're hired**

Describe the term 'stakeholder'.

A vampire hunter.
Buffy being the most famous

Hugo King is an engineer. He is a sole trader.
Explain the business term 'sole trader'.

It means he has sold his sole
to the devil!

What is a 'partnership'?

A Ship that takes two people to drive

John's net pay is £150. His deductions are £38.
a) Work out John's gross pay.

The money he spends on porn magazines every week.

b) State one mandatory deduction from John's pay.

Beer

c) State one voluntary deduction John may or may not pay.

Tax

Claire used good body language at a job interview.
Can you think of three examples of good body language
that Claire may have used.

1 pole dancing

2 The moonwalk

3 The Bolero

Claire was well prepared for her interview.
Explain how Claire may have prepared herself for the
interview.

Had a bath and put on her
lucky pants.

Subject: ......**Psychology**.....................

I think, therefore ...

Describe what is meant by 'forgetting'.

I can't remember

Explain a religious theory for the existence of the world.

The big bang was God dropping something

Outline with two examples what is meant by 'unanswered prayers'.

1 **Not winning The Lottery**

2 **Arsenal never winning the league**

Freud stated that the superego contains the moral aspect of one's personality. Define the term 'superego'.

A really fast sports car

Explain the 'psycho-dynamic approach'.

Using your Mind to Move things
.like a Jedi

Suggest a way to abate aggression.

If your hands are tied behind
your back you can't punch people

Explain the process of 'learning'.

A process by which information goes into one ear and out of the other.

Express the term 'stereotype'.

It is what kind of CD player you own.

What does the phrase 'case study' mean?

It is a process whereby you sit and stare at your suitcase before you go on holiday but not knowing what to pack.

Using your knowledge of Freud, provide an example of when a dream represents Freud's theory.

If you dream about biscuits it means you are subconsiously thinking about sex, but if you are dreaming about sex, it means you are thinking about biscuits.

Who said 'I think, therefore I am'?

I did.

Please fill in the sections of Maslow's Hierarchy of Needs below.

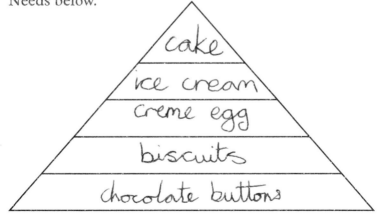

Subject: **History**

What was introduced in the Children's Charter of 1908?

Children

Name Labour's first cabinet minister.

Mr Chippendale

Where was the American Declaration of Independence signed?

At the bottom.

Name Britain's highest award for bravery.

Probably Nelson's Column

Upon ascending the throne the first thing Queen Elizabeth II did was to…

Sit down

What was Sir Walter Raleigh famous for?

He is a noted figure in history because he invented cigarettes and started a craze for Bicycles.

Summarise the key developments of the Industrial Revolution.

Industry revolved

How did Christopher Columbus discover America?

While he was cursing about the Atlantic

Name one of Abraham Lincoln's greatest achievements?

Having his pace carved in rock

Summarise the major events of the Cold War.

It started off by someone throwing an ice cream + then someone threw a lolly back.

What were the consequences of the Cold War?

Everyone got really hot what with all that running, fighting in the snow with snowballs and riding horses pulling sledges. No wonder Father Christmas has rosy red cheeks.

Why was the Berlin Wall built?

Germany was competing with China.

Who were the Bolsheviks?

People led by linen

Explain the word 'autocracy'.

A country that has lots of cars.

Explain what is meant by the word 'dictator'.

Someone who reads
out loud

Why did Britons have better health after the year 1990?

Because the eighties were
over

What was the largest threat to world peace in the 1980s?

Heavy metal, because it was very loud.

Explain what happened during the Night of the Long Knives.

People all over Germany planted their knives in the garden at 7pm and the next morning they had all grown to ridiculous lengths.

What did Mahatma Gandhi and Genghis Khan have in common?

Unusual names

What does The Statue of Liberty represent?

A green lady holding up a large glass of wine She is wearing a crown. She is the Queen of America.

Name two of the classes which existed in Medieval England.

History class &
Geography class

Subject: General Studies

Redundancy is often an unpleasant and unexpected event in someone's life. Give two examples of unexpected life events.

1 death

2 reincarnation

Fred has many friends. They all enjoy playing football and drinking in the pub. Fred drinks over 40 units of alcohol each week but the recommended limit is 28.

Explain how Fred may be affected by:

a) playing five-a-side football

If he drinks before football he is unlikely to score (goals or girls)

b) drinking 40 units of alcohol each week

He doesn't have much money left at the end of the month

Sally has recently been promoted at work and she received a pay rise. Sally decides to get a credit card for non-essential spending. Can you think of three examples of non-essential purchases Sally may use her credit card for?

1 toilet roll

2 marmite Flavoured crisps

3 Gucci handbag

Employees at 'Bob the Baker's' have to wear plastic hats or caps. Why do you think this is?

To stop headlice from jumping into current buns

Jeff has been asked to collect data about the amount of television his friends watch.
Think of an appropriate question he could ask them.

How much TV do you watch?

What guarantees might a mortgage company insist on when buying a house?

They may check to see whether you are well endowed before allowing the purchase.

What is a co-operative?

It is a shop which is not as expensive as M&S

What happens during a census?

During the census a man goes from door to door and increases the population.

Subject: .... *ICT* ....

What is a computer virus?

An S.T.D.
A systematically Transmitted Disease.

Joanna works in an office. Her computer is a stand-alone system. What is a stand-alone computer system?

It doesn't come with a chair

What is hacking?

A really bad cough

The local swimming pool uses a computer system to regulate the water level. Can you suggest a disadvantage of using a computer in this instance?

Computers do not make very good lifeguards.

Can you think of two reasons why Hazel would rather receive an email as opposed to a letter?

1. She doesn't like her postman

2. She hates paper cuts.

Suggest two advantages for shopping online.

1. You don't have to have that horrible "it doesn't fit" moment in the fitting room.

2. You can do it in your pyjamas.

Suggest an advantage to video conferencing.

You can't smell bad breath via video

What is malware?

It is badly made clothing

What is a CD-ROM?

An album of romantic music.

What is a hard disk?

It doesn't break when you put it in the dishwasher.

What is a floppy disk?

It is a disk that has been left
at in the rain

What is a network?

When you chat to people you
don't like to try and get a job.

What is a palmtop?

The leaves of a tropical tree

Give three professions where palmtops are a useful tool.

1. Coconut picker

2. Basket maker

3. Somebody who flaps palm leaves over their boss to cool them down.

What is a desktop?

Where you do your work

What do you use to navigate a desktop?

A map and a compass

Subject: **Religious Studies**

What is the significance of an altar?

God knows.!

Christians only have one spouse, what is this called?

Monotony

What do Christians celebrate at Christmas?

When Joseph and Mary had a baby called Jesus. They travelled to Bethlehem by plane and Pontius was their pilot.

What were Jesus' closest group of followers known as?

The 12 decibels

What miracle do Christians celebrate at Easter time?

Chocolate!

Other than Christianity, state two religions.

1 The Force in Star Wars

2 Football

What is the difference between the New Testament and the Old Testament?

The New Testament was a better version.

What is a pilgrimage?

It's when lots of people wander off in the same direction for no apparent reason

Who was Solomon?

He was a very popular man who had 700 wives and 300 porcupines

Subject: *Classical Studies*

Name one of the early Romans' greatest achievements.

Learning to speak Latin.

Name the successor of the first Roman Emperor.

The second Roman Emperor

Write what you know about Nero.

A really good coffee shop.
Starbucks was his main competitor.

What were the circumstances of Julius Caesar's death?

Suspicious ones

Where was Hadrian's Wall built?

Around Hadrian's garden

What is Spartacus known for?

He was famous for leading a slaves'
rebellion in Rome and later he became
famous for appearing in a blockbuster
movie all about it.

Name the wife of Orpheus, whom he attempted to save from the underworld.

Mrs Orpheus

Who was it that helped Theseus escape from the Labyrinth?

David Bowie

Who wrote *The Republic* and *The Apology*?

Play-doh.

2p, or not 2p?

Subject: **English**

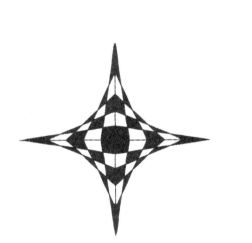

Discuss the style of *Romeo and Juliet.*

It is written entirely in Islamic pentameter.
The play is full of heroic couplets,
one example being Romeo + Juliet
themselves

How does Romeo's character develop throughout the play?

It doesn't, it's just self, self, self,
all the way thrash.

How much is Romeo to blame for what happens at the end of *Romeo and Juliet*?

He is completely to blame.
He's an alpha male and
he's named after a car.

Use the word 'judicious' in a sentence to illustrate its meaning.

I am using 'judicious' in this
sentence to illustrate it's meaning

Imagine you work for a travel agent. Describe a place you have been to and explain why it would interest someone of a similar age.

My mum and dad drag me to Butlins every year. I wouldn't recommend it to anyone my age.

Why should we be optimistic about the future? Use either a discursive or an argumentative style in composing your answer.

Because if you're not positive about the future then you ain't got much hope have you.

In *Pride and Prejudice*, at what moment does Elizabeth Bennet realise her true feelings for Mr Darcy?

When she sees him coming out of the lake.

Suggest an appropriate word for each of these meanings:

a) An appliance or implement designed to help one do work.

My parents and the Internet

b) To be on water without sinking

Jesus

c) Aggressive; harsh

My brother and my teacher Mrs Topley

d) Faultless or highly-skilled

My answers!

BLACKBOARD BLUNDERS

Spelling Slip-ups and Homework Howlers

I ♥ SCHOOL

mrs Pearson said I could stay in at playtime and help her sick up some pictures on the wall.

The headteacher likes to snivel around on a black chair in his office.

My teacher said I was very epidemically bright. I was prowed!

The scool hell is being painted so we had assembily in our classroom.

If you are really naughty you get exploded from school.

The teacher looked at Mark and growled,
'I expose you think that's clever!'

When we did the coin game I
was the looker and Mark was
the tosser.

We was playing futbol and we fell and we started to have a fit. It was not a bad fit but the teacher tolled us of.

Once there was a dog in the playground and we went to smoke it but the dinner lady told us to keep away.

Yesterday, Bert asked if he could burrow my football shorts at break time.

There are lots of birds in the school garden. The other day I saw some tits and a chaffage. The chaffage was pink and grey.

Teecher saud I couldn't do PE because I hadn't brot my pimps.

My favorit game at playtime is stock in the mud and playing with the dope. I can use a skiping dope on my own.

We wieghed the school rabbi today. it was two killer grans. When he becomes four killer grans, we haf to put him on a diet.

When PC Handley visited he had a helmet and a smart white shit.

The teacher in deception class looked across the room and shouted 'Slop that at once!' That was a surprise.

I am very very sorry. It is wrong to keep giving massages to my friends when I should be listening to the teacher. I will not do it again.

I found a spare seal so I quickly sat on it.

In the playground we play docters and and nurses but I got told off. I got told off because Henry had a sore throet and I put a stick on his tunge to see inside. The stick was from a tree.

I scored the winning goat in our football match, the minger was really impressed.

MINGER

ME

THE ARTS

Today I painted an octopuss with big eyes and eight purple testicles.

Lowry's pictures were mostly about the different prats of Manchester.

I'm good at sewing, I will be able to run up curtains soon.

You have to boo early for the
school play.

I love drawing and painting
so my favourite subject is ars.

I luv J. K. Rolling, she is my heroin.

When you write a story you should do a daft copy first. Then you can change it round and make it sound better.

If you don't want to use a full stop you can use an exsitement mark instead.

'You are under a rest and you will be remembered in custard for the night,' said the policeman. He wasn't expecting that!

In the next part of the story, the judge condomned the prisoner to death.

The pilot was bound to crash the plane. The moment he saw his wig come loose and fall to the ground he knew there was no chance of survival.

'And now' declared Mr Scarlett-Jones 'I shall read your uncles last will and testacle.'

The two cars sped down the road. The crooks had stolen the Jagger but the police were catching up fast with there top of the range Grandad.

She went mad and they put her in the menstral institution.

Robert was In a very bad crash and he has not wocken up from it.
I think he is in a cromer.

The driver flashed at me so I decided to cross the road.

There was an acident on our road last night and a man was badly enjoyed.

Time seemed to be standing still. Nothing was happening and I was getting scarred. I looked again at my cock. It hadn't moved since I last looked at it.

The whistle sounded and smoke paumed from the ship's flannel.

The magician tapped on his majik box and said 'abracadabra' and then varnished from under the table.

'Look at your hands!' said Mrs Grumble. 'I don't know where you've been but they're as black as the arce of spades!'

As he stepped outside he gave a quick nob of his head and everybody knew what he meant.

There was a very thick frog on the
roads last night and it maid a
car crash into a bus.

Mr. Brown walked into the room and sat on his favourite choir.

In last year's ~~many~~ Christmas concert, Linzi played the main prat. I played one of the smaller prats and I would like to have a bigger prat this year.

... and at the end of the show we all sing away in a manager.

When my big sister palyed Glodilocks I was aloud in the concert too. I just had to be a little bare.

GEOGRAPHY

The north pole is so cold that the people that live there have to live sumewhere else.

You use the 24 hour clock in summer because it stays light longer.

The closet town to France is Dover. You can get to France on a train or you can go on a fairy.

In geography we learned that countries with sea round them are islands and ones without sea are incontinents.

They used to think the earth was fat but it is really round. It is shaped like a spear.

In Scandinavia, the Danish people come from Denmark, the Norwegians come from Norway and the Lapdancers come from Lapland.

A flat map of the world is an atless.
A round map is a glob.
Globs are more intresting.

I feel sorry for children in Africa. They are staring to death. They only get a little groin to eat. I would not like to eat the groin.

We lernt about africa in geography class, I would like to see the wild breasts roaming the plane.

A ship's window is called a pothole.

There are lots of carnivorous forests in Scotland. And in the forest you can see dears and slags.

MATHS

I need to work hard on my maths so I will be god at it.

We drew a giraf to show how many trafics went passed the school.

Frackchens are like harvs quarters and tirds.

I would like to be an accountant but you have to know a lot about moths.

Two halves make a whale.

The total is when you add up all the numbers and a remainder is an animal that pulls santa on his slay.

The most popular crisps were salt and vinegar and the least popular were ready slated.

if you gess but you dont gess hiy enuf Yu undress to mate.

If it is less than 90 degrees it is a cute angel.

SCIENCE

One of the most important farces is the farce that pulls things to the ground. This farce is called gravy

A snog is a kind of dirty fog. It is made by plution. In some countrys they have snog every day and peopol even have to wer masks to stop it from hetting them.

Today our teecher tort us about the new Hardon Collider — when it's turned on it could corse a big bang.

YOU CAN GET AN ELECTRIC SHOCK FROM A PYTHON AND BE KILLED.

Helicopters are cleverer than planes. Not only can they fly through the air they can also hoover.

Our solar system is made of a sun, nine planets, lots of moons and balls of fire which fly around inside the system and can cause damage. These are called hemaroids.

If there are alons out in space I would like for them to come to earth and say hello. Or whatever yr i say if you are an alan.

We can all see things because we have a septic nerve that joins our eyes to our brians.

The sun rises in the east and sets in the west. That is why it's hotter in the east.

Computers have made our lives easier. But sometimes do not. They often break down And we get sperm-mail.

HISTORY

Sir Walter Raleigh circumcised
the world with a big clipper.

my favourite subject is history.
i like looking into the post to
see what i can find.

If you had no money in the 1930s you could get some by going to the porn shop. The man at the porn shop had 3 balls hanging over his entrance.

Then Joan of Ark met her end. She was burned as a steak.

We buy poopies and weare them all week. On poopy day we all go quiet and think about dead people.

In the olden days cars were not aloud to go fast. The first cars had to follow a man with a fag in his hand.

For the Frist time in history people could have mashines to help them with their work at home You could have a Frig in your kichen.

In wartime Children who lived in big cities had to be evaporated because it was safer in the country.

If you did something brave in the war you might get a meddle.

florence

Sugar Lump

Florence Nitingale was known as the lady with the lump.

In the oldern days the streets were very bumpy because they were full of cobblers.

SOMETIMES IN THE WAR THEY TAKE PRISNERS AND KEEP THEM AS OSTRIGES UNTIL THE WAR IS OVER. SOME PRISNERS END UP IN CONSTERPATION CAMPS.

Captain Cok was a famos exploder. He siled the seas in his sailing ship.

There are two houses of parliament in our country. The main one is the house of Comons. The other is the house of lords.

I had traveled back in time to the war, I tried to buy a drink but I only had new money on and it was going to cost me a shilling. What could I do?

In the field near our house they think they have found the remains of a Roman fart.

After the war they had to build houses quickly to replace the ones that had been bombed. These houses were called perverts. There are still some old perverts around today.

The sultanas had wifes
and also porcupines

The Easter game of egg rolling
started in deberhams and cornwall.

Dico dansing started when my mum was young. Before that there was lots of other danse fashons. In the 1920s there were girls called floppers...

Greek Gods

The three gods in my project are the king of gods – Zeus, the messenger of the gods – Hermes, and the god of war – Arse.

The sufrajets complaned
for voles for women.

WHAT I
DID ON MY
HOLIDAYS...

On our activity holiday Dad wanted to ride the hores, but mom said they were too ekspensiv.

We spend two weeks in grease every year.

My uncle Steve took my cusins to Blackpool to see the aluminashons. We went to Blackpool as well but we went to see the lights.

We nearly ran over a peasant in the weekend. It ran out from a framyard.

This holiday we got some slobs to make a patio in the back garden.

Some of the biggest fish my dad had caught are from our holidays. He has caught pikes and craps.

Wen we were in fotland we used to go into the woods for a walk. Dad liked to see how many bees he could see.

When it gets neer Cismas I get choclat penis. I get one evry morning.

Santa carries all the toys in a big sock on his back.

Last chrismas I herd Santa putting the presents in our living room. He nocked over something and swored like daddy.

It was peek season when we went on holiday to the beach; there were ladies in bikinis everywhere.

this is a pikstur of my mum sellin speyds.

RELIGIOUS STUDIES

Dear God,
My wish is that there wood be pis all
over the world. Make the wars end and
and let pipol live in pis all their lives...

The church near my hous is three
hundred years away, we go there
on wholly days and Sindays.

Jesus died cross, he had bleeding feet and he was stoned.

If you marry two people you are a pigamist, but morons are allowed to do this.

I did a cak stall for charity, i sold all my caks. The Cristian charity was a non-prophet organisation.

A mosque is a sort of church. The main difference is that its roof is doomed.

In jewish churches they do not have vickers. Insted they have rabbits.

Jesuses dad was josepf. He was a crapinter.

Adam was lonely so he made Eve out of a apple tree.

The most famus of the ten commendments is thou shall comment on a duckery.

Monks are men who give their life to God and marry nuns. They live in a monstery.

I asked my mum why we said old men at the end of prayers at skool, I don't know any old men apart from grandpa.

All over the world there are different religons. The people dress different and do different things but one thing is the same. They all worship agog.

NATURAL HISTORY

Every living thing is an orgasm. from the smallest cell to a whole mammal, there are orgasms everywhere.

In Australia they have small kangaroos as well. They are called wallies.

Baby cows are chars and baby bulls are bollocks.

My hobby is insest. I lern about all kinds of insest from a book I bort at the bring and bye sale. I speshly like aunts.

Ostralia is famos for its speshal animels like kangeroos, cola bears and cookerbuggas. You carnt get this anywuer els.

The best place to put pants is somewhere warm and damp, where they can live happily.

That is the end of my project on porkypines. My next one will be about armydildos.

we have to look after the sky.
poolution can spoil it and so can spraying
too many arsols.

I like to pik up smells on the beach
and keep them in my room.

Crap rotation is what farmers do when they have grown the same crap in a field for a long time.

Crabs and creatures like them all belong to a family of crushed asians.

The jungles of Africa are very dangerous for the people who explore them. There must be hundreds of people who have been mauled to death by a tiger or lino.

... and there are monkeys with red bottoms called buffoons.

Fax hunting is cruel. Faxes can be a bit of a newsance at times, specially if they come at night but it is still wrong to get crowds of people and dogs to rip the poor little faxes to shreds. I think fax hunting should be made iligitimate.

FOOD

Every morning dad has a slice of dread before he goes to work.

Last week it was Jack's berthday. He bront a cak to school and we all had a pis. I had a pink pis.

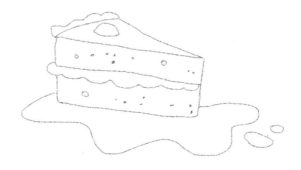

The best dinner is spagete bolonase. Its main ingredents are pasta, sause and minge meat.

All our family love sweats. I like sticky buns with icing on top but my mum is the worsed. She loves bras of chocolate. She had three chocolate bras on friday evening last week.

When we go and see my
nan she always gives
us lots of nise things
to eat. My mum has a
current bum and I have
a batenball cake.

We got our tea from the chinees last night. I love ommimental food.

They couldn't fit us in for a meal at the restraint because we hadn't reversed a table.

On speshal ocashuns i am alowed coke.
My dad has wiskey. He says its
his farrit nipple.

You can make toste by putting
bread in a toster or by putting it
under a girl until it is done.

I FEEL SICK!

I went to see the docter because I keep getting orful crap. I woak up with the crap all down my leg yesterday and I cuddent put my foot down.

The densits sicked a sicker on my frunt for being gud.

If you feel portly go to the nurse or docter.

I brock my tooth and I had to get a feeling from the dentist.

Safety is very impotent. My brother was unsafe on his bikcycle and he fell off and broked a bone in his back called his cockstick.

I keep getting whacks in my ear and it makes me a bit def. I think the docter will try to suck it out.

I was scarred of going to the bentist but I just felt a little prick and went to sleep.

Sometimes if you are reely reely poorly you go to a speshal ward in hospital and the ward is called insensitive care.

After I saw the school nurse I felt butter, on the hole.

My brother broked his humorous bone in his arm, he had a plaster put on and a large slong.

HOME TIME

I hepled my dad in the garage. He let me hit some nails in with his hamster.

for my praty we went to the blowing alley. When we had been blowing we had a drinck and a burger.

At brownies this week we ~~beer~~ lernt to do sin language. I lernt fensing too. Fensing is when you fight with a sod.

...and then Mr. Browning showed us how climbers use tampons to grip on to their roc.

. . . and tow times a week we have a nashonal lottery. There are six balls and a boneless ball.

I go to St Johns to lern fist aid. I have lernt how to do a bondage and I got to practice on Mr Terry. He is the leader.

I take the dog for a walk in the park every morning.

The girl who collects our rent has stopped coming. Now we have a rent boy instead

My tummy rambles after school so I have ✱ choclet suggestives when I get home.

I saw some grillers at the zoo, they werr big and herry like my dad.

My mum falled down the stairs and was lying prostitute on the ground.

My mum saw my messy bedroom and said it was abdominal. I felt a lot of quilt.

Dad talked about weapons of mass digestion while eating dinner. I'm worried about this — I don't want to get bumbed.

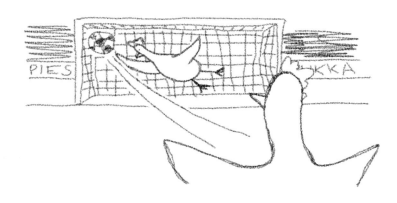

My dad luvs watching the footy — he says it's poultry in motion.

I used to not like our pet dog because he was viscose, he has groaned on me now.

My mum keeps ghosts in our garden,
they keep nippling the washing.

We had a swimming pull dug in our
garden and my dad filled it with
his big nose.

FRIENDS AND FAMILY

my grandad has got ahuye orgun. he says one day he will give it to me but I have to lern how to play it.

This wikend we went shoping. I got some new shoes and mummy got a new pair oy tits.

When I was foul, I had a speshul party and a cak which I shaved with all my firends.

Mum and dad were panting in my bedroom this weekend. They panted it blue and stuck a cute boarder round the middle.

Mummy had been in the bath and when she dryed her
her hair she saw her bush was missing. We all lookd
gor it but daddy let her have his comm.

I have lots of fiends at school and I
have even more fiends at home.

and I took a bunch of violents home for my mum.

We have faund out that anty Mary is stagnant and she will be having a baby in March.

The funny thing about my family is that they are all divers. My uncle Tim is a taxi diver, my uncle Steve is a bus diver and my Dad is a van diver.

My mum goes to jim every fireday.
She always comes home too tired to do
anything.

We went to visit my dad's boss this holiday.
He lives in a big hose.

Every time we go shopping we have the same fuss. Dad wants to read the Mirror and mum wants her Daily Male.

We took my baby sister to the panto for the frist time this year. We went to see Seeping Beauty.

We are taking my little sister to see Satan this weekend.

On Sunday my dad filmed me falling into our pond by axident. We are going to send it to You've Been Farmed.

Dad was working in the garden and he ~~was~~ ascked mum if she could come and give him a hard. She was bisy so aunty jo went instead.

My mum was a bit shook up yesterday because she had a dump in the car.

Since her axident my mum has to go to a
fizzy therapist every week.

My uncle is impotent.
He is the boss of a big factory.

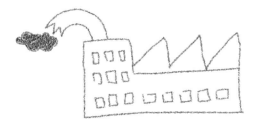

Mummy givs chang for the slat
mashins and baddy is a dinga
Calver.

My gran has a huge chest. We keep our
toys in it.

my uncle jake died last week and he still isent better.

Grandad aront let me have his old programmes because he wants to keep keep them for his pasterior.

My dad took me dog racing on sunday, my favrit was a cocky spaniard.

WHEN I GROW UP

I like sewing. I would like to be a Sewer when I grow up. I am helping my mum make a pachwork kilt.

when I grow up I want to learn how to tipe quickly and I want to be a tipissed.

I would like to be a signtist and I would like to work in a lavatory.

My uncle shouts at my cussins and makes them do chors. One day they are going to be polisemen and polisewomen so they can put him in prison.

I wuld like to be a vet becouse I enjoy meating animals.

My sister is a babyseller. She gets
money from the groun ups, and sells
their babys while they are away.
I would like to be a babyseller
too.

WHEN I AM OLDER I WANT TO
██ LEARN TO DRIVE A CAT.

I would love to have lots of babys when I'm a grownup. My mummy says I have to wait untill I'm much older but tina across our road has lots of babys and she isnt grownup. She also has lots of husbends.

I am going to be a scientologist because I am cleaver at science.

My dad wants me
nurse but I want to be a dancer.
I can do both. Work in the day
time and a dancer in the
He says this could be true because he
once knew of ladys who did that.

BEDTIME

My sister is 3. When she goes to bed she calls her blanket a wanket. It makes my mum and big sister larf.

I dident get to sleep mutch because next doors dog was baking all night.

My little sister still has to sleep with the
Light on because she is afraid of the dork.

Befor i go to bed i sometimes hav a mug ful of
warmed up milk to help me go to sleep. Mummy has
Mug ful of wine.

My dad works nights so he spends all
day in deb.

My baby bother sleeps in a cat in my bedroom.

It is verry noisy at night for me because we live above a pube.

... and suddenly the door opened and banged against the wall. I felt a lamp in my throte.

I sleep in my bedrom. My broter sleeps in his bedrom. My mummy sleeps in hers and daddys bedrom but daddy sumtimes sleeps on the sofa with our dog. I think this is because he grawls like a dog when he is snooring in his sleep.

Sam's mum looked at her little boy. 'Come on, it's up to the land of nob for you.' she said.

Kids' Klangers

The Funny Things That Children Say

Out and About

When passing a racetrack in the car:
Child:

What goes on there?

Parent:

It's where people race horses.

Child (after some thought):

I bet the horses win.

Girl:

Can I go and play with those boys outside?

Mother:

No, you can't, they're a bit rough when they play.

Girl:

But if I find a smooth one, can I play with him?

Mum at a toddler group to her small child when she spies some other mums looking her way:

I think my ears are burning.

Child (looking anxiously at her mum):

Quickly, put them out then!

Sweet-looking little girl says to colourful caterpillar found on the ground:

Aw, lovely little caterpillar... (stamps on it) THERE! You're dead now!

Child:

Daddy, I really need the toilet!

Dad:

OK, we'll stop soon. Do you need a number one or a number two?

Child (thinks about it for a while):

I need a twelve!

On seeing a headless tailor's
dummy in a clothes shop:

I'll pray for you.

About a house that only had the
wooden framing done:

Oh, I wouldn't want to live in
a house like that – it's naked!

Daddy, if you close your eyes when you drive, it makes you go faster!

Little Girl watching her father fall over as he tries to demonstrate how to roller-skate:

Mummy, what's Daddy doing now?

On the way out of an expensive shop, and in a loud voice:

Mummy, are we leaving because you don't have enough money to buy anything?

I went to Kenya for my holidays. I went not to have a safari adventure, but a family one. We went because all my family lives there... except my mum, dad, my brother, me and my sister.

On seeing a sign for no dog fouling:

What does that sign mean?
No smoking for dogs?

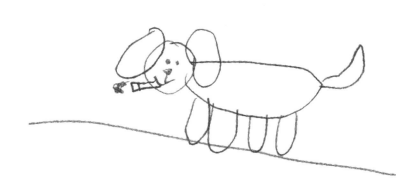

On seeing a dark line in the sea
from the plane window:

Look Mum, there's the EQUATOR!

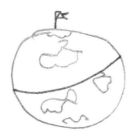

Seeing a police dog in the
back of a police car:

What did he do?

When going into the toilet block
at an amusement park:

What ride is this, Mum?

About the GPS system in the car:

How does she know where
we are going?

Parent:

Look at that lovely German shepherd over there.

Child:

How do you know he's German?

To a bobby on the beat:

Oh my gosh, does your mum have to help you put those big boots on?

A little girl had wet her knickers and been told by her mother not to worry because it's just an accident. The next week while out shopping, she turns to her mummy and says:

I really need an accident!

Mum, I want to go on a cargo ship, you know, one that the car goes on!

A father and child were in an antiques shop looking at teddy bears. The dad had a bear at home from his childhood called William that was badly showing its age. The small child, being aware of the threadbare state of the bear goes up to the very snooty saleswoman and says in an earnest voice:

My daddy's Willy is going tufty.

When seeing people riding bicycles:

Don't their feet get dizzy?

For my holidays I went to Euroland and met Snow Wipe and Sleepy Booby. I met Mickey Mouse – he is a real mouse.

A mother and small child were at the funfair. The child is delighted with his mum's efforts on the 'Hook a Duck' stall and shouts with pride:

My mum is the best hooker!

I paid for my sweets myself. I went up to the lady and she put my pennies in her castrator.

After seeing their first
ever ballet performance:

Why were they on tiptoe all the time?
It would have been easier if they
just used taller people.

I'm not going in the car with Dad
– he drives like a ninny.

Pointing at a gravestone:

Mummy, do people live in there?

When I Grow Up

I would like to be a cow or
a girl when I grow up.

When I'm big, if I have a baby and
it's a boy, I'm going to have to sell it,
because boys are really horrible!

I'm going to be a superhero and save the world. I'm going to go and do 1,000 push-ups in my room now.

I think I want to be a dragonfly when I grow up. Or a dentist.

I want to be just like my daddy when
I get big, but not with so much hair
all over. I'll probably have hair on my
bottom just like my dad, too.

I want to be a teacher because I
want to be allowed to wear
high heels all day.

When I grow up I want a really massive house with spider legs.

I want to be a policeman, so I can arrest my daddy when he puts me on the naughty step.

I want to be a penguin so I can play outside all day.

I want to work with commuters because I'm good at pressing buttons.

Child:

I want to be a pirate when I grow up
so I can fly the plane to Disney World
and meet Mickey Mouse.

Parent:

It's a pilot that flies a plane,
is that what you mean?

Child:

Can pilots wear eye patches
and peg legs too?

I want to be a fish except I've never seen one. Do people eat fish?

I want to be a celebrity chef like Gordon Brown.

When I grow up I'm going to shave my arm pips.

I'm not sure if I want to grow up. Will my bones fall out like my teeth, so that bigger ones can grow?

Animals and Pets

Make sure that you never blow in a cat's ear because if you do, usually after three or four times, they will bite your lips together! And they don't let go for at least a minute.

Electric eels can give you a shock.
They live in caves under the sea where
I think they have to plug themselves
into chargers.

A dolphin breathes through its bottom
on the top of its face.

Sharks are ugly and mean and have
big teeth, just like my big sister. She's
not my friend any more.

My parents took me to the zoo at the
weekend. My favourite animal
is a fricken elephant.

Child:

Dad! I think our cat is dead!

Dad:

How do you know that?

Child:

Because I pissed in its ear.

Dad:

YOU DID WHAT??

Child:

You know... I bent down and went psssssst in its ear and it didn't move.

Why do cow yards smell like poo?
Don't they know how to flush?

A little girl's puppy wanders into the bathroom when she's in the bath.

Girl:

No Mum, he can't come in!

Mum:

Why? He's only a little puppy dog.

Girl:

But he's a BOY puppy!
And I'm naked in here.

Did God mean for giraffes to look like that or was it an accident?

My puppy still has stinky breath even after I gave her a Polo mint.

A preschooler speaks to his dad about some newborn kittens that he went to see with his mum:

Boy:

There were two boy kittens and one girl.

Dad:

How could you tell?

Boy:

Well, the woman who owns them picked them up and looked underneath – I think it's printed on their bottoms.

I saw a hedgehog and
it had pickles all over it.

Never wear yellow outside because bees and wasps will chase you. They think you're a dandelion.

A small child when collecting eggs in the morning from the family's chickens:

Can we get some pigs, then I can collect the bacon and sausages in the morning too?

Crabs can hurt because they have little princes that can nip you.

We went to a farm and the farmer pointed out his prize bollock. It was really big and steam was coming off it because it was a cold day.

My dad taught me about lemons. They jump off cliffs to their deaths. I would not like to be a lemon.

My Family

Little girl threatening younger sister:

If you're going to do that, you'll have to face the quenchy-quenchies!

My mummy is the best, and I love her so much that as soon as she's dead I'm going to bury her underneath my bedroom window.

Two children overheard in the playground
discussing what their parents do for a living.
First child:

My dad is a postman and
my mum is a teacher.

Second child:

My dad is an old codger – at least
that's what my mum says he is, but I'm
sure what one of those is.

Whenever your mum is angry and asks you, 'Do I look stupid?' it's always best not to answer her.

Mummy, when you're dead, can I have your slippers?

Don't let your mum brush your hair
when she's in a bad mood
with your dad.

Always ask your grandparents for
something if your mum and
dad have said no first.

Why don't grandma and grandpa have names like the rest of us?

A grandfather is a man-grandmother.

A little boy after seeing an ultrasound:

My mummy is having a baby. I know because I saw it on the telly!

On seeing grandma's false teeth in a glass by the side of the bed:

I can't believe it! How much is she going to get from the tooth fairy for all of those?

A child after seeing his parents'
wedding photos:

Is that when Mummy came
to work for us?

Small child to grandma:

Are you older than my other nana?
Does that mean you'll die first?

I'm glad you're not deaf, Grandma.
Because then you wouldn't hear
the funny things that I say.

My dad taught me that you must only
use swear words when
using a hammer.

My mum told me she is stagnant,
I hope I get a baby sister.

Indignant child to their grandmother
after being told off:

Well I don't care what you say,
because every night you sleep next to
my granddad and cuddle up
to him like a big wimp!

Sunday School

God spoke to me one night. He said 'Rmmrrm!' But it might have been a lawn mower or a motorbike.

What did God stand on when he was creating the Earth?

I am not really a Christian.
I believe in fairies and pixies.

Child (pointing to a dead bird in the garden):
Daddy, what happened to him?
Dad:
He died and went to heaven.
Child:
Did God throw him back down?

Angels don't eat but they drink milk from holy cows.

Child:

God! God! GOD!

Mum:

What's the matter?

Child:

I'm just talking to God. Why isn't he talking back to me?

Our Father, Who does art in heaven, Harold is His name.

And lead us not into temptation,
but deliver us some email.

Child:

Grandma, do you know how
you and God are alike?

Grandmother:

No, how are we alike?

Child:

You're both really old.

God looks after us when we are
sleeping because he has a special
key and just lets himself in.

The seventh commandment is
thou shalt not admit adultery.

The greatest miracle in the Bible is when Joshua told his son to stand still and he obeyed him.

A small child was looking at an old Bible in his parents' house and very carefully turning the fragile pages. Someone had used the book as a flower press at one time and out fell a few leaves and flower heads. The stunned child shouted to his mum:

Look! I think I've found Adam and Eve's underwear!

It was a miracle when Jesus rose from the dead and managed to get the tombstone off the entrance.

Jesus was born because Mary had an immaculate contraption.

Angels live in cloud houses made by God and his son, who's a very good carpenter.

After a wrong number:

Mum, who was on the phone?
Was it Jesus?

When we go to heaven we get to live
with Santa and Rudolph in the sky.
That's where my hamster went.

Angels work for God and look after
all the children when God is
busy with other things.

Looking at headstones in a cemetery:

Are those the Ten Commandments?

Overheard in church:

Oh come let us ignore him
Oh come let us ignore him
Oh come let us ignore him
Price that lawn.

God created Adam and Ebay.

God is really old and wrinkly,
kind of like a dinosaur He-Man.

A small child to a shocked mother on
the way home from school:

Milly and Jane said that their parents
are Roman Catholic, so I told them
that our family are all prostitutes.

Today I learned about doughnut and the whale in Sunday school – doughnut was eaten by the whale because he'd been bad. He was a bad doughnut.

A small child and his father are standing at the entrance to the church after matins and are looking at a war memorial.

Child:

Daddy, what's that?

Dad:

It's a memorial that's dedicated to those who have died in service.

Child (wide-eyed):

What? The service this morning?

Dinner Time

On being told that sausages
are made from pigs:

You can't eat pigs – they're
the farmer's pets!

I have chocolate flavour milk at
bedtime. And Molly (pointing to her
baby sister) has booby flavour.

I think beer must be good. My dad says the more beer he drinks, the prettier my mummy looks.

Can I have sprinklers on my ice cream?

A boy opens a box of animal-shaped biscuits and empties them out all over the kitchen table:

Mum:

What on earth are you doing?

Child:

It says on the box that you shouldn't eat them if the seal is broken. I'm trying to find the seal.

My mum's a virgin because she doesn't eat meat.

Child after having a piece of popcorn extracted from his ear:

Doctor

Why did you put the popcorn in your ear?

Child:

I didn't put it in there...
my ear sucked it up!

If turkey comes from turkeys,
does ham come from hamsters?

I love toucans on my soup. They're really crunchy but also a bit chewy and get stuck in my teeth.

Explaining the difference between
an item of food and a dish:

A carrot is a carrot,
but macaroni cheese isn't.

Mummy, long ago, did you have food?

On seeing sesame seeds
on a burger bun:

This has hamburger seeds in it!

After having some microwave beans:

That's the best meal you've
ever made me!

I used to believe that when I ate all my dinner up that it went down to my toes. Now I know it only reaches my knees.

Before people landed on the moon, everyone thought the moon was made of cheese. It's actually made of rock, but that's what happens to cheese when you leave it out of the fridge for too long.

Asked if they've had chicken pox:

No, but I've had Cocoa Pops.

Small child when asked what
their favourite vegetable is:

Chocolate!

I love going to the cinema
and having cop porn.

Being green means eating more orgasmic vegetables, because they're better for you.

I'm not having grilled cheese sandwiches. Boys only eat boy cheese sandwiches!

That was spicy. It hurt my feelings.

Small child when asked why they
are not eating their dinner:

I've lost my apple tights.

A small child was helping to bake a cake.
After breaking the eggs and eyeing
up the electric whisk she says:

Can I make the eggs dizzy now?

Small child who has eaten too much:

Mummy, my cheese is biting back!

My dad isn't very well today
because of his overhang.

School Days

When Robert brought his Action Man into school it was constipated, because we're not allowed to have toys in school.

Who draws the lines around the countries?

A fossil is something really old. It sometimes contains the footprints of a fish.

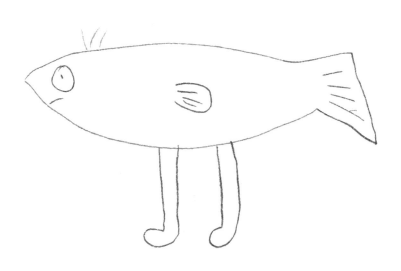

Elbow grease is what you use to make things clean. You can only use it when you have a scab on your elbow, otherwise there's no grease.

Dad:

Did you enjoy your first day at school?

Child:

Not really, I had to stay awake all day!

We've got a spinach girl coming to stay. I won't know what to say to her, though, because I don't know spinach.

I learned how to do colouring-in in deception class today.

We made a leaving card for Mrs Bow because she is retarded at the end of term.

If you are surrounded by sea you are an island. If you don't have sea all around you, you are incontinent.

When teachers get old, like over
forty, they're always in
a really grumpy mood.

In a geography class:

Thunder is a rich source of loudness.

Most of the houses in France are made of plaster of Paris.

It used to be Mummy who took me to school, but now we have a big new bust that takes us.

A buzzard is when it snows sideways, but tomatoes are even more dangerous – you can see them coming from miles off and they can wreck houses and lift cars off the ground.

You can listen to thunder after lightning and tell how close you came to getting hit. If you don't hear it you got hit.

Talc is found on rocks and on babies.

I've been told I can take violence lessons in my music class, except I'd rather play the piano.

Christmas

The three wise men brought the baby Jesus some presents of gold, frankincense, myrrh and silver. But I think he would have preferred some Star Wars action figures.

There was an angel at Jesus' birth called Gabriel. All he did was fly around a lot.

I think Jesus was born in a shed, or a barn, or a stable – one of the three.

They followed a special Christmas star, which is only out in December.

Jesus's mummy and daddy are called Jovis and Mary.

Is the Frankie Scents
like men's perfume?

A small child when inside a
church for a carol service:

Where's Carol then?

After counting down to one we all shouted happy new ear.

Overexcited child on Christmas Eve, while putting out a mince pie and sherry for Father Christmas:

Oh I know – why don't we leave him half the turkey as well?!

The Birds
and the Bees

When are you going to tell me about
the birds and the Bee Gees?

Love is what happens when a girl
puts on perfume and a boy puts on
aftershave and they go out together
and smell each other.

Child:

Is your belly button a door that your baby comes out of?

Mum:

No.

Child:

Phew, because that would really hurt!

When you love somebody, your eyelashes go up and down and little stars and rainbows come out of you.

A small child asking about
how babies are made:

How do you find the bones for them?
Are they lying around somewhere?

If we started life as a tadpole why am I not a frog? It's not fair.

A child talking about his baby brother:

First, Mum and Dad made him as a symbol of their love, and then Dad put a seed in Mum's stomach, and he grew in there. He ate for nine months through an umbrella cord.

Will I lay eggs when I'm a grown-up?

When asked what a midwife does:

She delivers babies, but she doesn't have a sign on the car like the Domino's man.

I'm not sure how the egg gets there to begin with, but I think it comes from food. You have to eat very healthy food, even like eighteen broccolis a week.

How are mothers made?

God made my mum just the same like he made me. He just used bigger parts.

What Do You Look Like?

My grandma is a very nice lady but her skin doesn't fit her face.

To a cashier:

You have such lovely yellow teeth.

Mum! Daddy's hair is missing
off the top of his head!

Small child to grandma:
You look like a very pretty man.

Mummy, I'm sure you were taller last year.

Small child to sweaty daddy:

Why is your face leaking?

Child:

Mum, you've got boobies.

Mother:

Yes, I have.

Child:

All mums have got boobies haven't they?

Mother:

Yes...

Child:

Why has daddy got them then?

Mother, on seeing her child
with food round her face:
Just look at your face! To which the
confused child cries: I can't!

My baby sister looks like a volcano
about to burst when she has wind.

Small child pointing to a woman in a cafe:

Mummy, do all women grow moustaches?

Mum, you'd look so much better if you rubbed out those lines on your face.

Child on seeing his mum
applying make-up:

Why are you drawing round your eyes?
Is it so you don't lose them?

What Love is All About

On seeing a couple kissing:

He seems to be whispering
in her mouth.

If grown-ups are in love, they are
all dressed up. And if they are just
wearing jeans and a T-shirt it might
mean they just broke up.

I'm worried about what will happen with my bed when I get married. How will I fit my wife in?

If you're not wearing your ring, someone else might try and steal you!

When a person falls in love for the first time, they fall over, and they don't get up for at least an hour.
It can really hurt!

If falling in love is as hard as learning how to write, I don't want to do it.

Make sure you're good at kissing by the time you get married, so your wife won't mind if you never do the washing up.

Married people always hold hands when walking down the street to make sure their rings don't fall off, because they were very expensive.

My mum says it's best to find someone who is kind. That's what I'll do. I'll find somebody who's kinda tall and kinda handsome.

When people get married they promise to go through sickness and diseases together.

If it's your mother, you can kiss her whenever you like. But if it's someone new, you must ask them first.

Marriage is when you get to keep your girl and don't have to give her back to her parents.

On seeing a couple kissing:

I think he's trying to steal her lunch!

Home Time

Mum:

Is that a party invitation?

Child:

Yes, but I can't go because it says 2 to 4 on it and I'm 5.

While watching TV with her mum, a child passes the remote control and says:

Here you go, Mum. You can be Daddy.

A mum was feeling a bit tearful after a hard day looking after her two small children. One child says to the dad who has just walked in:

Is she teething?

I love watching the adverts. My favourite is the one with the Durex doggy.

A little boy keeps on playing with his willy in the bath, so his mum tells him not to play with it or it might fall off, to which he replies:

What, like yours has?

Have you seen my favourite gloves? They are stripy, and they are shaped like my hand.

Will you play hide and seek with me?
I'm going to hide under my bed,
so don't look there.

Parent:
Why are you not replying to me?
Child:
My face is asleep, be quiet!

Frustrated with a childproof cap:

How does it know it's me?

Small child on being told her
friend had broken her arm:

What, right off?

Can we watch Star Tracks?
I love Jean Luc B'stard.

When asked what they would do if
there were no parents:

We could eat chocolate cake
whenever we wanted to!

American child to English babysitter:

I wanna go potty.

English babysitter (misunderstanding):

Oh you want to go to a party? Parties are fun, aren't they?

Child:

I wanna go potty!

Babysitter:

Yes but we have to go and meet your parents now sweetheart.

Child (rolls eyes and sighs with exasperation):

No silly, I gotta go to the bathroom!

Child:

I can't sleep because there's a
monster under my bed.

Mum:

Don't be silly, it's just your imagination.

Child:

What's my imagination
doing under there?

Mum:

You did a brilliant job of putting your
sandals on except they are
on the wrong feet.

Child:

But I don't have any other feet, Mum.

Showing her mum a rash:

Look Mum, I've got heat raddish!

Little girl called Grace:

Hail Mary, full of Suzanne...

Mother:

No, it's 'full of grace'.

Grace:

I know, but I thought my sister might like a turn at having her own special prayer named after her!

Dad:

I'm going to teach you about building a fire – do you know what you can burn on a fire?

Child:

Wood and paper.

Dad:

That's right – and what about coal?

Child:

What, like Cheryl Cole?

← Cole

After falling out of bed:

I wasn't watching where
I was sleeping.

A parent calls home and after a few
rings their child answers:

Hello.

Parent:

Gosh, you sound out of breath.

Child:

No, I have more.

A little girl had a pet tabby cat called Alice.
One day she saw a strange white
cat in the garden and said:

Look Mummy, there's a
white Alice outside!

A penny for your socks, Dad.

Child:

Mum, I want an 'orse.

Mum:

You want a horse?!

Child:

No I want oars to row my boat with.

On being told to behave:

I am being have!

If you're interested in finding out more about our humour books, follow us on Twitter: @Summersdale

www.summersdale.com